ISBN: **1502305860**
ISBN-13: **978-1502305862**
LCCN: **2014921219**
Create Space Independent Publishing Platform
North Charleston, South Carolina

"... what we found was that rather than being haphazardly arranged or independent pathways, we find that all of the pathways of the brain taken together fit together in a single exceedingly simple structure. They basically look like a cube. They basically run in three perpendicular directions, and in each one of those three directions, the pathways are highly parallel to each other and arranged in arrays. So, instead of independent spaghettis, we see that the connectivity of the brain is, in a sense, a single coherent structure."

Van J. Wedeen
a Harvard neuroscientist and physicist.
A study at the Massachusetts General Hospital
Funded by the National Institutes of Health,
March 2012.

ACKNOWLEDGEMENTS

I'd like to express my gratitude to the following people who provided me with knowledge, inspiration and the vision to write this book.

To Ray Kurzweil, futurist, author, inventor and visionary. His book, **The Singularity is Near**, inspired me to write this book. He helped me understand the relationship between the computer and human intelligence, and his research exposed me to advances in artificial intelligence and voice recognition.

To Phil Savenick, author, artist, director and filmmaker. I was honored to visit his home which features a museum of television history and a shrine to Philo Farnsworth, the inventor of television. He helped me understand the intimate relationship between computer monitors and television.

To my wife Monica, for her patience while I was consumed by the creation of this book. Her perspective and insight brought me up to a level that I could not have achieved on my own.

Table of Contents-I

Prologue

Where did counting begin? Perhaps with notches on bones thousands of years ago. Were these notations perhaps etched to count seasons, kills, or children?

The origins of mathematics accompanied the evolution of social systems. Many social needs require calculation and numbers. As and organized, the need to express quantity emerged.

Society eventually emerged from hunting and gathering to mostly agrarian communities. Counting probably arose spontaneously more or less independently from place to place, and tribe to tribe. Various number systems arose, remarkably similar.

The transition from counting with markers to counting with mechanical devices occurred over thousands of years. society realized that records of accounting were required, statistics were saved and archived. Scientists came along and developed logic to accompany counting, and the early computer was born.

2030 – Will Computers Become Human?

More recently, the arrival of remote control devices, gave rise to the field of robotics. Soon computers became autonomic, with sensors in and responses out. In June of 2014, IBM simulated a brain on a chip...

Who first conceived the idea that someday computers would "think" in ways that one could not distinguish from a human? Perhaps it was Alan Turing. Born in 1912, this British mathematician, cryptanalyst *(in World War II),* computer scientist and marathon runner, created the concept and first model of a general purpose computer. It became known as the Turing Machine.

More germane to this book is his prediction that computers would someday "think" so similarly to humans, that if a problem was posed to a human in one room, and a computer in another, the questioner could not distinguish from which room the answer came from. He predicted that this would happen within 50 years with a 30% success rate. Although his prediction did not materialize, recent breakthroughs in artificial intelligence have convinced me that, by 2030, the 30% "indistinguishable" rate will be achieved or exceeded.

Part I. Evolution

How did computers evolve?

How will they be transformed?

Let me take you on a journey…

I-1. Counting and Numbers

Before 1810, little was known about "computing" other than the use of counting devices dating back to the ancient abacus. In 1804, Frances Jacquard developed a fully automated loom that was programmed by an early version of the punch card. By 1820, Charles Xavier Thomas de Colmar created the "Arithmometer", the first commercially successful calculating machine, which remarkably could add, subtract, multiply and divide.

In parallel with the stages of development of the computer was the evolution of number systems. It all started when humans had reasons to count. Animals count their young, and birds desert their nests when more than one egg is taken from them.

Ancient Incas, a highly advanced civilization, had no written language but developed the Quipu counting system, a system where thin strings were looped around a larger cord. It is believed that this was the first base-10 numbering system.

Ancient Egyptians had an understanding of fractions. They wrote fractions with a numerator of 1, but used hieroglyphics for the denominator. Their numbering system was a base-10 system with a unique sign for every power of 10.

The Babylonian system is one of the oldest systems, dating back 5,000 years. It was a system of wedge-shaped "tally" marks, and had a value depending upon the direction in which the wedge was pointing. The Babylonian system was the first symbolic system used to tell time of day.

The Mayan numbering system in the fourth century was perhaps a thousand times more advanced than the European system. They used a Base-20 system which had only two symbols, a dot and a dash. They were the first to symbolize the concept of zero.

The Greek numbering system, interestingly enough, was based upon their alphabet, which came from the Phoenicians.

The Roman numbering system, still in use today, was a rather static system which changed only slightly through time.

The base-10 decimal system is the most widely used system in the civilized world. Because it uses the digits 0 through 9 and powers of ten for the position of the digit in the number, it can represent any number, no matter how large.

However, the decimal system does not lend itself to logical processes, nor can it easily be integrated on a computer's processor *(or chip)*.

Instead, the binary system is a base-2 system and only uses two symbols, 0 and 1, called "bits". It represents logic as well, since 1 is true and 0 is false.

All data and logical operations within a computer's memory or processor is stored as a series of zeros and ones.

I-2. The Babbage Engine

Charles Babbage was born on December 26th, 1791, the son of a banker. He graduated from Cambridge University in 1810 with a keen interest in mathematics and an astonishing knowledge of calculus.

Often called "The Father of Computing," Babbage was an innovative thinker and a pioneer in the computing field. His knowledge of mathematics was so respected that he was hired by the Royal Institution shortly after graduation to lecture on calculus. Only two years later, he was elected a member of the Royal Society and along with his friends, founded the Astronomical Society in 1820.

By 1822, Babbage began to design a "difference engine", which is a mechanical calculator that tabulates polynomial functions. The engine itself consists of parallel tubular columns which must be precisely machined in order to produce error-free calculations. The machine used the decimal number system and was powered by a crank handle.

The British government became extremely interested in Babbage's engine, since producing tables of statistics was time-consuming, expensive and not always 100% accurate.

In 1822, Babbage presented a "difference engine" to the Royal Astronomical Society in a paper entitled "Note on the application of machinery to the computation of astronomical and mathematical tables." The British government gave Babbage £1700 and work on the project began.

Babbage's goal was to overcome errors in tables by mechanization. Every part of the engine had to be formed by hand using custom machine tools, which Babbage constructed.

The result was an engine that was able to calculate polynomials by using a numerical method called the "differences" method. Although his first engine, completed in 1822, produced discrepancies, it was far more accurate than earlier mechanical devices.

Babbage is considered to be the pioneer in computing, having developed the first mechanical computer and, later, the steam-powered machines that mechanized calculations of polynomials.

I-3. Boolean Logic

George Boole, born in 1815, was an English mathematician, philosopher and logician. He is considered to be the inventor of Boolean Logic, which is the foundation of the digital computer.

In 1849, Boole was appointed as the first professor of mathematics at Queens College in Ireland. His early works attempted to systematize the fundamental principles of Aristotle's logic.

Boole did not regard logic as a branch of mathematics. Instead, he proposed that logical propositions could be presented algebraically through the manipulation of symbols in equations. He is considered to be the inventor of computer programming.

The fundamental thesis for his logic consists of "elective symbols", primarily the logical operators "and" and "or" *(represent in formulas as "&" and "|")*. This, coupled with a base numbering system with the lowest level a 1 or a 0, is the essence of Boolean logic represented in algebraic equations.

His contributions to the algebra of logic were viewed as immensely important and influential in the development of computer processors.

2030 – Will Computers Become Human?

Boole conceived of the fundamental method of comparing "sets" by using just three operators: AND, OR and NOT.

Boole's novel approach (at the time) of using only two symbols *(1 and 0)* to represent opposites is fundamental in programming logic.

Boolean logic is used in computer programs *(i.e. software)*, as well as in computer hardware, in the form of 'gates'. Gates on a processor affect the flow and direction through a computer program. Gates are the logical "switching stations" on any computer.

But what *is* a "computer"? The fundamental architectural model was first described in June, 1945, by John von Neumann and it survives today *(but maybe not after 2030)*. The von Neumann model states that a computer consists of (1) a central processing unit *(CPU),* (2) an arithmetical and logical component *(ALU),* (3) mass storage, (4) a program "counter", and (5) input / output (I/O) channels.

Von Neumann also introduced in 1935 the concept of a stored program which would be placed into random access memory (RAM). Charles Babbage's Analytical Engine incorporated the von Neumann model and provided the ability to store a program consisting of punch cards, a concept based upon the Jacquard loom of 1801.

Von Neumann was probably the first to articulate the similarity between the computer and the brain. The output of neurons in the brain is essentially digital and sequential.

I-4. Hollerith's Punch Card System

Throughout history, civilized man has had a need to record information. The first evidence of the use of the number 1 seems to be about 20,000 years ago, when a uniform series of single lines was cut into the "Ishango" bone *(the fibula of a baboon),* was discovered by archaeologists.

Numbers and counting didn't come into extensive use until the rise of cities and commerce, around 4000 BC. When subtraction joined addition, arithmetic was born.

There is evidence of recording devices in clay cones that were stored in pouches. Later, these cones were replaced by marks on clay tablets. Ancient Sumerians recognized the need for people to keep track of "things"; this was the beginning of the accounting profession.

Around 3000 BC, the number **1** was transformed from a counting unit to a unit of measurement. Builders of temples and pyramids invented the cubit, probably the first standardized unit of measure.

Under the guidance of Pythagoras, the Greeks developed the concept of odd and even numbers. Later, another Greek mathematician Archimedes conceived on theoretical math, and his experimentation with math games led to practical use in the world of commerce and banking.

These accumulations of statistics need to be stored so that it can be recalled later from archives, and then analyzed.

The earliest medium for data storage was in the form of "punch cards" containing at first, round holes, and later rectangular holes. One of the first uses for round-hole punch cards was for toll tickets on U.S. East Coast turnpikes, in order to record the place of entry of a vehicle and to charge the toll upon exit.

As early as 1725, these cards with round holes were used for controlling textile looms. In 1890, Herman Hollerith developed the first punch card machine under contract with the federal government to process the 1880 census. His design was based upon the Jacquard loom, and the working system was completed in just three years.

2030 – Will Computers Become Human?

His machine saved the US government $5 million, a good part of the budget in those days. Hollerith later formed a company which today is known as IBM.

Interestingly, the 60 million cards punched in the 1890 census were fed *manually* into the machine. The counts for each column were displayed in dials on the face of the tabulator. A "sorter" attached to the machine would be activated by certain hole combinations and the result was a set of census statistics.

The remarkable growth of IBM in its early years is attributable in great part to the "IBM card", as the punch card came to be known. In IBM's first half-century, the data on punch cards held nearly all of the world's collected data.

The first computer programs were "written" by typing on a punch-card machine *shown below).* If a deck of cards was dropped, it could be sorted on a punch-card sorter *(shown below).* Program decks were read into early IBM mainframe computers, which filled a good-sized room .

Punch cards were the foundation of early mainframe computers, and extremely profitable for IBM.

In 1928, IBM transformed and standardized the punch card to be the exact size of a dollar bill, with rectangular holes and 80 columns, some of which would be used for sequence numbers in the event that the deck needed to be sorted.

A cottage industry was born, with rooms full of punch card machines, sorters and clerks who provided services for data entry and tabulation. These facilities came to be known as service bureaus.

With the advent of mainframe computers, cards were pre-formatted with sets of columns labelled with their specific purpose, as shown below.

I-5. Farnsworth's "Camera Tube"

In June of 2014, I was privileged to spend an evening with Phil Savenick at his home in California. Phil is a former Disney animation executive, filmmaker, artist and historian, and is one of the most fascinating persons that I have ever met.

At the center of Phil's home is a museum dedicated to television history, and a shrine to Philo T. Farnsworth, the pioneer of the technology that made modern television *(and later, PC monitors)* possible.

Philo, born in 1906, was raised in a poor home with no electricity. In 1919, his family moved to his uncle's 240-acre ranch near Rigby, Idaho, to sharecrop. Fortunately, the ranch had not only electricity but also a cache of science magazines like **Popular Science** in the attic.

Philo's thirst for knowledge opened up a whole world of creativity and inventiveness. One day, while driving a farm vehicle, Philo looked at the newly plowed field, and what he saw was evenly parallel lines, row after row. It occurred to him that an image on a "tube" could be sliced into parallel rows, and then each row could be transmitted in a continuous sequence. The "raster" image was born.

Peter A. Bornstein – The "30" Series

At age 14, he used a lens to direct light into a glass camera tube, and invented what was later known as a vacuum tube. In his chemistry class in Rigby, Idaho, Farnsworth sketched out his vacuum tube on a piece of paper.

Although neither his teacher nor his fellow students grasped the implications of his concept, he had created the fundamental architecture that would revolutionize television.

In 1926, he scraped together enough funds to continue his scientific work and he moved to San Francisco with his new wife, Elma "Pem" Gardner Farnsworth.

In 1927, Philo took a glass slide, smoked it with carbon and scratched a single line on it. This was placed in a carbon arc projector and shined onto the photo-cathode of his vacuum tube.

The following year, he unveiled his all-electronic television prototype *(the first of its kind)* that used a video camera tube or "image dissector." This was the same device that Farnsworth had sketched in his chemistry class as a teenager.

Between 1926 and 1929, Farnsworth was consumed by a lengthy legal battle with RCA and other corporate giants. He won the case in court, and his most convincing evidence was the sketch of his vacuum tube.

He was granted Patent #1,773,981 on August 25, 1930, for the cathode ray tube (CRT) which became the display for all black and white television screens in the early days of television, and he began to receive royalties from RCA and other manufacturers.

In 1930, his wife, "Pem" Farnsworth became the first television actress. In early television filming, she could not face the camera directly because the lights were so hot, and she was required to move away completely after only a few moments. Since the image was black and white, she used heavy makeup for contrast and emphasis.

By the age of 64, Farnsworth held more than 300 United States and foreign patents, most of which formed the foundation of the television industry as it swept the world and changed the nature of our society.

I-6. The First Non-mechanical Computer

The earliest calculators were mechanical and controlled by push-buttons or levers. They were driven by gears, cams, belts or shafts.

In 1937, J.V. Atanasoff, a professor of physics and mathematics at Iowa State University, built the first non-mechanical computer, called the Atanasoff-Berry (ABC) computer. It was the first automatic digital computer. A replica currently at Iowa State University is shown on the next page.

By 1941, Atanasoff and his graduate student, Clifford Berry, created the first "multi-tasking" computer that could solve 29 equations simultaneously.

The Atanasoff-Berry computer is sometimes credited with being the first to store information in its main memory. However, this computer was _not_ programmable. It was designed solely to solve linear equations.

There is some debate about whether the "Berry" was really the first digital computer. Some computer historians give this credit to John Mauchly and Presper Eckert, creators of the ENIAC computer.

Other noteworthy developments in this area:

➢ In 1937, George Stibitz of Bell Labs constructed a 1-bit binary "adder", which was one of the first binary computers.

➢ 1n 1943, a team *(that included Turing)* at the Government Code and Cypher School in England completed a machine dedicated to cipher-breaking, the first decryption machine used in World War II.

I-7. Early Mainframes

The earliest computers, called "mainframes", were designed and developed with architecture that included memory, a control unit (CPU), an arithmetic logic unit (ALU), and Input and Output.

In 1943-1944, the first electronic computer arrived. It was the *Electronic Numerical Integrator and Calculator* **(ENIAC)**, financed by the U.S. Army and designed by two University of Pennsylvania professors, John Mauchly and J. Presper Eckert. It is now considered to be the grandfather of digital computers. It filled a 20x40 foot room and had 18,000 vacuum tubes. It was digital and capable of being reprogrammed to solve a broad array of numerical problems.

The ENIAC was initially designed for the Army to calculate artillery firing tables based upon the ballistics of weapons at that time. The media portrayed it as "a Giant Brain", with a breakthrough speed *(at that time)*, of 1,000 times that of electro-mechanical machines.

Shortly after the end of World War II, the ENIAC was programmed to analyze the feasibility of the hydrogen bomb.

2030 – Will Computers Become Human?

In 1946, Mauchly and Eckert left the University of Pennsylvania and received funding from the Census Bureau to build the **UNIVAC**, the first commercial computer for business and government data processing.

The increasing demand for large computers was triggered when "second generation" transistors replaced vacuum-tubes in the late 1950s. This spurred development in hardware and software, but early manufacturers commonly built small numbers of each model, targeting narrowly defined vertical markets.

The **NEAC 2203** computer was one of the first transistorized computers. It was developed in Japan in 1960 for the purpose of managing Japan's Kinki Nippon Railways online reservation system. It supported both Roman and Japanese character sets, and may have been the world's first multilingual computer.

IBM was a pioneer of advancements in the power and capability of mainframes in the forties, fifties and sixties. The first automatic digital calculator in the United States, built for Harvard University in 1944, was named the **Automatic Sequence Controlled Calculator**.

Other significant computers in the IBM chronology:

- **1946**: the **IBM 603** Electronic Multiplier, the first calculator to be placed in production.
- **1948**: the successful **IBM 604** Electronic Calculating Punch.
- **1949**: the Card Programmable Calculator (**CPC**), the first IBM product designed specifically for use in data service centers.
- **1952**: the **IBM 701**, the company's first commercially available scientific computer.
- **1953**: the **IBM 650** Magnetic Drum Calculator, the largest selling computer in the 1950s, and
- ...the **IBM 702** Electronic Data Processing Machine, with data and programs stored on tape drives.
- **1954**: the Naval Ordnance Research Calculator (**NORC**), for many years the fastest computer in the World, and
- ...the **IBM 705** Electronic Data Processing Machine, successor to the 702, with twice its memory.
- **1956**: the **SAGE** (Semi-Automatic Ground Environment) AN/FSQ-7 series of computers, used for a quarter-century in the U.S. air defense system, and
- ...the **IBM 305** Random Access Memory Accounting Machine (**RAMAC**), which employed a magnetic disk memory unit for real-time "in-line data processing".

- **1958**: the **IBM 7090**, the first commercial airline reservation system, employing the proprietary **SABRE** software.

IBM's "big iron" Data Processing Division (DPD) was formed in 1956 to focus on the design, manufacturing, distribution and marketing of mainframe "super-computers".

Mainframes eventually gave way to mini-computers and word processing machines that could serve the needs of small businesses.

I-8. Programming Languages

Ada Lovelace, the daughter of poet Lord Byron, was born in 1815 and is considered to be the first programmer. Ada had a passion for technology and mathematics. Although she married an aristocrat, William Lord King, she always felt that her true soul mate was Charles Babbage. Babbage, while given credit for inventing the Difference Engine *(and later, the Analytical Engine),* was exasperated that the logarithm tables within these engines were fraught with errors and could not be relied upon by navigators, astronomers and bankers.

Ada enlightened a frustrated Babbage with her "Ada's Algorithm", which envisioned that the Analytical Engine could be applied to any process that manipulated data. Her translation of data into a process stored within an "engine" was truly the first programming language.

Unfortunately, Ada never received any remuneration for her algorithm, and only used her theory to bet on horses. She ran up huge debts and died relatively unknown at age 36 of uterine cancer.

2030 – Will Computers Become Human?

Ada's algorithmic concept led to the development of early programming "languages", such as Plan Calculus in 1945. The programs were actually "wired" into electromechanical computers and controlled by toggle switches on the computer's panel.

As mainframes became more widely used in most large and even mid-size industries, the need arose for in-house computer programming departments on which commerce, the military and government could rely. Resources for designing and developing programs for general purpose computers were in short supply, and early programming methods were at a very primitive level, mostly at the "machine" level. These initial methods employed constructs of ones and zeros (bits) as computer instructions .

Assembly language, first created for the EDSAC computer in 1949, is a low-level (binary level) programming language that was first input to mainframe computers on punch cards or magnetic tape. Typically, a single program would run on a 1940s computer and multi-tasking did not exist.

Programs were written in very elementary instructions and then converted to executable machine instructions by utility programs called Assemblers.

Because of the need to write commercial programs at a much higher level, early programming language developers recognized the need for English-like high-level languages.

Grace Hopper led a team at Remington Rand in 1959 that developed **COBOL**[1], the first commercial high-level programming language. It was the first user-friendly business-oriented programming language.

Once COBOL programs were entered from data entry devices, they were stored on media and then compiled, and converted into machine language. However, unlike the assembler, a single COBOL instruction would expand to hundreds, if not thousands, of machine instructions in the computer.

Almost immediately, COBOL standards were established by the American National Standards Institute (ANSI) so that input to compilers on any mainframe computer would be standardized, while the output of the compiler was dependent upon its manufacturer and design.

COBOL was designed for the development of business applications, and typically processed files on tape drives, or on large portable disk drives.

---

[1] Common Business-Oriented Language

A fault in the language not realized until the 1990s was that many COBOL programs were written to store the year as a two-digit number. As a result, most large companies scrambled during the 1990s to hire "Y2K" teams to convert all programs and data to 4-digit years. The teams were so capable that the predicted doomsday on 1/1/2000 never occurred.

In the mid-fifties, it was recognized that mathematicians and scientists required a more algebraic and formula-oriented programming language, and **FORTRAN** *(FORmula TRANslator)* was born.

In the late 1940s and early 1950s, John Backus at IBM assembled and guided a team of young men and women with a specific goal: to develop a programming language that could solve mathematical problems. His team consisted of a cryptographer, a chess wizard, programmers, mathematicians and engineers.

FORTRAN was designed for iterative processes, or "loops", that continued until an intended result was achieved.

In 1975, Backus was awarded the National Medal of Science, and two years later, the prestigious Turing Award *(see page 7.)*

In 1965, The **PL/1** programming language was released by IBM. PL/1 was developed by IBM at its Hursley, England development lab.   Prior to its release, PL/1 was employed exclusively for internal manufacturing applications.

PL/1 brought to programmers a mix of COBOL's business-programming capabilities and FORTRAN's mathematical and scientific functions. Like COBOL, it is procedural and English-like. Like FORTRAN, it is used for numerical computation, scientific computing and even systems programming. One of its strengths is bit and character string manipulation.

Programming for the Internet

The most widely object-oriented programming language is **Java**. It is used to combine snippets of code (*Objects*) into interactive web pages. With Java, *Procedures* in main-frame programs are replaced by *Objects*. Java is reliable and employs dynamic run-time error checking. A lot of emphasis is placed on security.

Javascript, on the other hand, is the most used language for interactive web pages. The programs are essentially *scripts* which run on a user's browser and respond to user actions such as mouse-clicks or timing of events.

PHP is the king of server-based languages used on the internet today. It runs on 75% of all web servers. Unlike Javascript, the program is written in HTML and the code is processed before it reaches the browser. The user sees only the final page.

I-9. The Chip Emerges

From the UNIVAC to the desktop PC, computers continue to process at an ever faster rate and have become remarkably smaller. A major contributor to this transition was the replacement of the vacuum tube with the transistor.

The type of vacuum tube used in early computers was a triode, invented by Lee de Forest in 1906. It was comprised of a cathode and a plate, separated by a control grid, and suspended in a glass vacuum tube.

The control grid controls the flow of electrons in either direction. By making it negative, electrons are repelled back to the cathode. When positive, electrons are attracted to the plate. It was an effective on-off switch (the "gates" described in I-3), but it consumed excessive power and gave off tremendous heat. In addition, these tubes were unreliable and failed often in large computers.

The transition from tubes to transistors has proven to be a game-changing contribution to the evolution of the computer as we know it today. The transistor was invented in 1947 at Bell Laboratories by engineers John Bardeen and Walter Brattain. It was a very reliable solid-state electronic switch, considerably smaller than the tube, and gave off little heat.

In 1948, Bell associate **William Shockley** invented the bipolar junction transistor (BJT), which relied on two types of semiconductors for its operation. BJTs can be used as amplifiers, switches or oscillators *(for timing of events)*.

Later on, many BJTs were combined in large numbers onto integrated circuits, invented in 1958 by **Jack Kilby** and **Robert Noyce**. Integrated circuits later came to be known as computer chips, deriving their name from the slice (or chip) on which they are built.
In 1964, Douglas Engelbart developed a prototype for the modern computer, with a mouse and a simple graphical user interface **(GUI)**. This transition marked the evolution of the computer from a specialized machine for scientists and mathematicians, to a technology that is more accessible and user-friendly for the general public.

In 1970, the newly-formed Intel Corporation unveiled the Intel 1103, the first Dynamic Access Memory **(DRAM)** chip.

I-10. Moore's Law

Moore's law is the observation that, over the history of the modern computer's design and manufacturing, the number of transistors in a dense integrated circuit doubles approximately every two years, at a constant price point. His prediction has proven to be quite accurate if,for example, you compare the Intel 4004 processor in 1971 having 2,300 transistors, with the Intel 486 processor in 1989 having 1.2 million transistors.

Gordon E. Moore (born January 3, 1929) graduated from the University of California, Berkeley, in 1950 with a B.S. degree in Chemistry. He earned his PhD in Chemistry, with a Physics minor in 1954 at the California Institute of Technology.

He began his career as an academic at CalTech, but soon left the Institute along with seven other alumni *(collectively known as the 'traitorous eight')* to form Fairchild Semiconductor.

In 1968, Moore and fellow engineer Robert Noyce, unhappy at Fairchild, decided to leave the company and start their own venture. On a single sheet of paper, Noyce outlined what would become the first Intel chip and convinced Arthur Rock, an early venture capitalist, to raise $2.5 million to fund the company, which they named the Intel Corporation.

2030 – Will Computers Become Human?

Intel pioneered the design, development and manufacturing of microprocessors. As of 2014 Intel is the largest computer chip producer in the world and dominates the market. Its market share in 2012 was 65.3%!

Moore's law has proven to be quite accurate, even in today's rapidly changing technology. It is still a guide in the semi-conductor industry for long-term planning and setting targets and goals for research and development.

The capabilities of digital electronic devices, regardless of industry, correlate remarkably with Moore's law:

- Microprocessor prices
- Memory capacity
- Robotic sensors
- Number and size of pixels in digital cameras

I-11. Personal Computers

The early 1970's witnessed a transition from mainframe and "mini-computers" for business, to personal computers mass-marketed to consumers. Earlier "microcomputers", developed in the 1950's and 1960's , were used for educational or experimental purposes, such as:

- The **Simon** in 1950, the first assembled digital computer, which sold for $600.
- The **IBM 610**, built between 1948 and 1957 at Columbia University, the first "Personal Automatic Computer (PAC)" to support floating point arithmetic.
- The Soviet **MIR** series of computers, developed between 1965 and 1969 was employed for engineering and science applications. It's processor contained a high-level programming language, and had an innovative graphic user interface (GUI) that included a keyboard, monitor and light pen.

The Xerox Alto was one of the first general purpose personal computers, designed for individual use. It was expensive and not based on a microprocessor, but rather. Using a "desktop metaphor" and a GUI, it greatly influenced the design of personal computers in the decades to follow.

2030 – Will Computers Become Human?

The Altair 8800 was the first <u>truly</u> personal computer. It was designed and developed in 1974 by hobbyists, and used the Intel 8080 chip. After being featured on the cover of Popular Electronics, it was sold by mail order. The designers hoped to sell a few build-it-yourself kits to hobbyists, but instead sold thousands in the first month. The assembled version could also be purchased and this was targeted to small businesses. This product ignited the micro-computer revolution.

The Tandy/Radio Shack TRS-80, launched in 1977, was one of the earliest mass-produced personal computers. Affectionately called the "Trash 80", it was designed with the Z-80 micro-processor. It was popular with home users, hobbyists and small businesses. It was sold at 3000 Radio Shack stores for around $600. Forecasted sales in the first year were expected to be 3000 units. However, it sold 10000 in its first year, and over 200,000 in its lifetime..

The Commodore PET *(Personal Electronic Transactor)*, mass-produced in 1977, was a top-seller in educational markets. It was built around a MOS Technology 6502 micro-processor. It was intended to bring on the demise of the calculator.

The PET was the first all-in-one-box home computer. It featured expansion ports for additional memory. Complaints about its calculator-sized "Chiclet" keyboard and unreliability resulted in commercial failure.

The IBM 5100 Portable Computer was introduced in 1975, six years before the introduction of the IBM PC. It was based on the "Scamp" prototype developed at IBM's Palo Alto Scientific Center in 1973.

It is considered to be the first "portable" computer, with an integrated keyboard, 5" CRT display, tape drive and processor.

In 1976 **Steve Wozniak** designed the **Apple I** computer while working with the computer hobbyists group Homebrew Computer Club. It integrated the Motorola 6800 processor instead of the far more common Intel 8080. It was the first computer with a single-circuit board.

Wozniak's friend **Steve Jobs**insisted that they start a company to sell these machines, and Apple Computer was born.

In 1981, IBM launched its first personal computer, model number **5150**. Because of its popularity, the term "PC" now referred to a desktop micro-computer compatible with IBM software, predominantly the Microsoft's MS-DOS operating system. It has an Intel chip, two floppy disks and an optional color monitor. Unlike Apple, the IBM PC used open architecture, which allowed other manufacturers to build expansion slot peripherals.

The Desktop Metaphor

The "desktop metaphor", first envisioned at Xerox PARC in 1970, is the unifying concept of graphical user interfaces (GUIs) that help users more easily interact with the computer. This concept has prevailed for decades.

It treats the computer monitor *(screen)* as if it is, in fact, the user's desktop, upon which *objects* such as documents and folders can be placed. Any document or folder can be opened in its own window, to be managed or edited. Accessories *(now called "apps")* such as a calculator or notepad are available in separate windows. The concept has been expanded to include gadgets, usually present on the desktop permanently or as a drop-down, such as a weather station.

Documents in this metaphor are usually presented in a paper paradigm, black text and a white background.

The mouse, keyboard and storage devices round out the early metaphor. Recently, touchscreen have been added to enhance or replace the keyboard. USB connections provide "plug and play" access to a wide array of devices that connect to the desktop. Wireless (WiFi) and Local Area Connections (LAN) now connect the desktop to the internet and beyond. But the basic concept of the desktop metaphor remains.

2030 – Will Computers Become Human?

Part II. Transformation
The Turing Test

When will a computer become human? In 1951, the British mathematician Alan Turing proposed that, if a person of either gender were in one room, and a computer were in another room, and a "judge" could not determine (most of the time) from which room the response to his questions came, artificial intelligence could not be distinguished from human intelligence.

The movie "The Imitation Game" refers to Turing's test and was released in 2014. The movie portrays the life of Turing, starring Benedict Cumberbatch as Turing, and Keira Knightley as Joan Clark, his star crypto-analyst.

Turing is credited with "breaking" the German's **Enigma** encryption machine. His software and brilliant design, implemented in the **Colossus** computer, was a vital contribution to the Germans losing World War II.

II-1. Futurists

Futurists over time have transformed the classic computer from a machine that sits on a desktop or one's lap, into a device that has senses and emotions, responds to sensory input, acts based upon its built-in logic, and *(in some cases)* performs its operations without human intervention or control.

The **Futurist** movement originated in Italy in the early 20th century in the form of artistic and social ideas. It glorified concepts of a future with high velocities, advanced transportation, futuristic industrial societies, and uncontrolled violence. The Futurists portrayed their concepts and predictions in almost any medium including painting, sculpture, theater, architecture and even gastronomy.

Futurists first organized in 1966 when the World Future Society was founded in Bethesda, Maryland in 1966. It is a non-profit organization that investigates how social, technological and economic advances are shaping the future. Through its magazine, The Futurist, and regional and national conferences, the society seeks to raise awareness of societal change, and promotes development of creative solutions.

2030 – Will Computers Become Human?

Ray Kurzweil, mentioned throughout this book, is the "Futurist-in-Chief" at Google. He is best known for the books that he has written on artificial intelligence, transhumanism, singularity and futurist movements.

Let's explore those areas of interest to modern futurists:

Artificial Intelligence is explored in the next chapter.

Transhumanism is cultural and intellectual research and thought that predicts the ultimate transformation of the human condition through available technology that will enhance the intellectual, psychological and physical capacity of human beings. These advances are expected to overcome human limitations, but are fraught with ethical concerns and even the fear that "posthumans" will eventually control humans.

Singularity is explored in chapter **II-6. Ray Kurzweil: Singularity** on page 79.

The Futurist magazine each year since 1985 selects the most thought-provoking ideas and forecasts of their members. Many of these visions are well "outside the box".

Here are some of some of the Futurists most interesting forecasts since 2006:[2]

1. Thanks to big data, the environment around you will anticipate your every move.
2. We will revive recently extinct species.
3. By 2020 populations will shrink, and wealth will shrink with them.
4. Doctors will see brain diseases many years before they arise.
5. Buying and owning things will go out of style.
6. Quantum computing could lead the way to true artificial intelligence.
7. Phytoplankton death will further disrupt aquatic ecosystems.
8. The future of science is in the hands of crowdsourcing amateurs.
9. Fusion-fueled rockets could significantly reduce the potential time and cost of sending humans to Mars.
10. Atomically precise manufacturing will make machinery, infrastructure, and other systems more productive and less expensive.

Kurzweil predicts that, by the year 2050, **total** artificial intelligence will prevail. If he is correct, nanoscopic robots will move throughout our capillaries, essentially transforming us into partly non-biological humans.

---

[2] Detail on these predictions can be seen at
http://www.wfs.org/Forecasts_From_The_Futurist_Magazine

2030 – Will Computers Become Human?

II-2. Artificial Intelligence

Artificial intelligence (**AI**) is a concept where a machine perceives its environment through sensors and makes decisions or takes actions that maximize a successful result. This concept was introduced commercially in 1990 at the Massachusetts Institute of Technology (MIT) and found its way into homes as the Roomba vacuum cleaner.

Early research into artificial intelligence was highly technical and specialized, focusing on accomplishing a specific outcome. The evolution from a primitive robot to the self-driving car of 2015 demonstrates how far we have come, but the goals of AI research continue to focus on reasoning, development of a knowledge base, design and planning, learning, natural language processing (communication), perception, and the ability to manipulate objects. This field is based upon the goal that intelligence can be so precisely emulated in a machine that the machine will simulate a human. This raises the ethical concern of creating artificial beings endowed with human-like intelligence.

Greek mythology imagined "thinking machines" such as the bronze robot of Hephaestus, and Pygmalion's Galatea. Every major civilization believed in human likenesses with intelligence. By the 20th century, artificial beings were introduced in fiction, as in Frankenstein.

In the summer of 1956, academic research in AI was founded at a conference at Dartmouth College. Three attendees became the leaders of AI research for several decades. Their research produced astonishing results *(at the time)* such as computers speaking English. By the mid-sixties, research in the United States was heavily funded by the Department of Defense and laboratories or "think tanks" emerged throughout the world. Artificial intelligence is now used for medical diagnosis and even for surgery *(i.e., Intuitive Surgical's da Vinci robotic system)*.

Although research into AI in the late fifties focused on imitating human intelligence, the linguists philosophers, logicians and others at MIT explored cognitive science, a field aimed at understanding the mental form and rules that are the foundation of perceptual and cognitive abilities. Noam Chomsky's work has influenced research not only into AI, but also in the fields of cognitive science, music theory, political science and programming language theory.

2030 – Will Computers Become Human?

In 1979, exploration of artificial intelligence emerged in the form of a nonprofit society called the Association for the Advancement of Artificial Intelligence (AAAI). This society focused on advancing the understanding of the mechanisms that underlie thought and intelligent behavior, and how this behavior can be embodied in machines.

Most AI societies are partially funded by member dues and they seek donations and grants. AAAI organizes conferences, symposia and workshops, and publishes a quarterly magazine for its members.

The term Artificial Intelligence is believed to have been coined in 1956 by John McCarthy when he assembled the first academic conference on the subject at Stanford. He focused on applied mathematical logic in computer programs to support the concept of AI. He was part of development teams that built early programming languages such as LISP and ALGOL. In 1960, LISP became the programming language of choice for AI applications. His license plate frame read *"Do the arithmetic or be doomed to talk nonsense"*.

No one has ever disputed the computer's ability to process logic and arrive at a result. But most people will question whether a machine can *think*.

Significant advances have been made in AI over the past 65 years, particularly with search algorithms *(i.e., Google),* machine learning algorithms, and the mass integration of statistical analysis to understanding the world at large.

AI expectations always seem to outpace reality. Significant breakthroughs have been promised *"in ten years"* for the past sixty years.

After decades of research, no computer has come close to passing the Turing test, although IBM's Watson is getting better and better at playing chess. Further research is encouraged by the Loebner Prize established in 1995 and the associated Turing Test Competition, with a $100,000 reward for development of a system indistinguishable from a human.

2030 – Will Computers Become Human?

In an effort to build a computer that could win a game of chess against a *master*, two approaches evolved: Type-A programs, which would use pure brute force, examine thousands of moves, and use a min-max search algorithm to specify the next move. Or, Type-B programs which would use specialized heuristics and 'strategic' AI, examining only a few, key candidate moves.

The Type-A approach was successful in May, 1997, when an IBM computer called Deep Blue® beat world chess champion Garry Kasparov after a 6-game match.

Today, Type-A brute force programs are chosen over Type-B due to the exponentially increasing processing power of computer chips, and to vast data storage available in the cloud. The next frontier for Type-A programs will be to win at the ancient Asian game of **Go**. Whereas chess has a branching factor *(possible moves)* of 40, Go's branching factor approaches 200.

Expert systems, a subset of AI, attempts to model human expertise in one or more *specific* knowledge areas. These systems have three basic components:

> A cumulative knowledge base
> An inference engine to process input
> An input/output (I/O) interface to interact with the user.

Expert systems are characterized by:

❖ The use of symbolic logic rather than numeric calculations
❖ Data-driven processing
❖ A knowledge base for a specific area of knowledge
❖ Interpretation of its results in a way that is understandable and useful by the user.

The dreams of scientists and science fiction enthusiasts go far beyond artificial intelligence. We are currently witnessing remarkable breakthroughs, which will be presented in the following chapters.

The ultimate goal for artificial intelligence seems to be autonomic *(see page 78)* "thinking" devices that are free of human guidance or interference. It is expected that we will ultimately arrive at a point when devices provide spontaneous and unsolicited advice, knowledge and guidance to their "masters".

2030 – Will Computers Become Human?

Ray Kurzweil in his book **The Singularity is Near** (see page 68) predicts that when computer processing is equivalent to the speed of the human brain, we will have computers as intelligent as humans. Will this be in 2030? I think so. Will computers act like humans? I think not.

II-3. Robotics

Is a mechanical bird a robot? Back in 350 B.C., Greek mathematician Archytas built a steam-powered "Pigeon" that was history's earliest study of flight, and probably the first model airplane.

Along came Greek philosopher Aristotle 28 years later who wrote:

> "If every tool, when ordered, or even of its own accord, could do the work that befits it... then there would be no need either of apprentices for the master workers or of slaves for the lords."

> ...suggesting how nice it would be to have a few robots around, while envisioning singularity.

In 1495, Leonardo Da Vinci built a mechanical device that looked like an armored knight. The mechanisms inside, mostly gears and pulleys, were designed to amuse royalty and move as though there were a real person inside.

By 1770, Swiss clock makers, led by the inventor of the modern wristwatch Pierre Jaquet-Droz, created three dolls to entertain royalty, one that could write, another that played music, and a third that could draw pictures.

2030 – Will Computers Become Human?

In 1898, Nikola Tesla *(does the name ring a bell?)* built and demonstrated a remote controlled robotic boat at Madison Square Garden. Did he ever dream that a successor robot would be powered by batteries?

Now let's look at the evolution to the modern day robot with built-in artificial intelligence.

Robots in the 20th century

The person credited with introducing the word "Robot" in 1921 was Czech writer Karel Capek in his play **R.U.R.** *(Rossuum's Universal Robots)*. The Czech word "robota" means "compulsory labor".

Beginning in 1940, Isaac Asimov wrote a series of short stories about robots. The first was **A Strange Playfellow** (later renamed "Robbie"). In 1950, all of his short stories were compiled in a single volume **I, Robot**.

Azimov's most important contribution to the field of robotics was his **Three Laws of Robotics**:
1. A robot may not injure a human being or, through inaction, allow a human being to come to harm.
2. A robot must obey the orders given it by human beings except where such orders would conflict with the first law.
3. A robot must protect its own existence as long as such protection does not conflict with the First or Second law.

The employment of the third law, while ignoring laws 1 and 2, is demonstrated by *Hal* in "**2001-A Space Odyssey**" *(see page 72)*.

In the 20th century, and even more rapidly in the 21st century, robotic technology has advanced rapidly and now robots can assemble other machines, and some robots can be mistaken for human beings.

The robot in the mid-20th century was seen as a curiosity, even appearing on the Tonight Show in 1966. Before long, robots found a place in industrial manufacturing and spread rapidly to Japan, South Korea and throughout Europe. In the mid-sixties, the first operational industrial robot in North America worked in a candy factory in Kitchener, Ontario.

Robots have found a place in other vertical markets, such as toys and entertainment, military weapons and search and rescue. Some even became "self-repairing" such as W. Grey Walter's Elmer and Elsie *(aka "turtle robots")*, which found their charging station when their batteries were low *(1948)*.

A major milestone in force feedback *(haptic[3])* technology was Raymond Goertz's first tele-operated articulated arm *(1951)*.

George Devol and Joseph Engelberger, in 1954, are credited with designing the first *truly* programmable robot. Named UNIMATE, it became the launch product for their company, Unimation, believed to be the first company to manufacture and market robots. The company is still in production today.

In 1957, the Soviet Union surpassed the United States by creating Sputnik I, the world's first autonomous artificial satellite.

---

[3] **Haptics** is the science of applying tactile sensation to human interaction with computers. A **haptic device** is one that involves physical contact between the computer and the user, usually through an input/output **device**, such as a joystick or data gloves, that senses the body's movements.

Research laboratories dedicated to producing robots with human-like artificial intelligence sprung up in universities. Among the first were teams at MIT, Stanford Research Institute (SRI), Stanford University and the University of Edinburgh.

Carnegie Mellon established the Robotics Institute in 1979, dedicated to integrating robotic technologies into everyday activities. They are a leader in innovate research in diverse robotics-related fields, and sponsor many academic programs from grade-school summer camps to PhD curricula.

In the late sixties, *walking* robots *(some with arms)* hit the scene. Breakthroughs included:

- A remote-controlled walking "truck" by R. Mosher.
- SRI's "Shakey", a mobile robot equipped with a vision system and controlled by a room-size computer.
- The Stanford Arm, which was the first successful computer controlled robotic arm.
- WAP-1, the first biped robot with artificial muscles, that could turn while walking and climb up and down stairs.

2030 – Will Computers Become Human?

> ➢ The Russian Academy of Science's first six-legged walking vehicle. Why six legs? It was developed as a prototype for walking on rough terrain such as the Moon, and controlled by algorithms that responded to sensors such as degree of climb or descent, or relative position of each of its six legs.

The 70's and early 80's generation of robots focused on robots that simulated the limbs of a human being. Included in this generation are:

- ❖ (1973) The WABOT I, a full-scale anthropomorphic robot, with a processor that controlled limbs, vision and conversation. It was thought to have the mental ability of an 18-month old. (1973) Cincinnati Milacron's T3, the first commercial minicomputer-controlled industrial robot, used primarily for welding.
- ❖ (1975) Victor Schenman at Unimation developed the Programmable Universal Manipulation Arm *(PUMA),* used in many industrial operations. It's advanced design, flexibility and precision results in high quality industrial products with few defects.

- ❖ (1980) The WL-9DR "quasi-dynamic" walking robot, controlled by a microcomputer, takes one step every 10 seconds. It was designed for "plane walking", which includes straight walking, sideway walking and turning. The designer's goal was for the robot's movements to be as smooth and rapid as man's walking.
- ❖ (1981) The Titan II and III, a quadruped which can climb stairs.
- ❖ (1990) iRobot Corporation produces domestic and military robots, dedicated to making a difference in people's lives. It's most well- known products in the nineties are the Roomba *(vacuum cleaning),* the Scooba *(floor scrubbing)* and the Braava *(floor mopping).*

2030 – Will Computers Become Human?

Robots in the 21st century

In the 21st century, robotics products emerged to support business efficiency, collaboration and the replacement of workers with mundane jobs. A leader in R&D for these commercial products is iRobot Corporation, moving from vacuum cleaners to video collaboration, and the world of "bots".

The 21st century products include:

- **Ava 500**, the Video Collaboration Robot. It's monitor on a pedestal allows business associates to establish a physical presence from a remote location with complete freedom of movement.
- The **RP-VITA® Remote Presence Robot**. It gives the medical community remote presence for patient care that combines autonomous navigation and mobility from the **iRobot** with telemedicine technology from **InTouch** Health.
- The **iRobot Ava Mobile Robotics Platform**, a solution suitable for 3rd party development and a wide range of applications. It is capable of autonomous navigation in complex real world.

- In 2014, Lowe's introduced robotic shopping assistants, the first retail robot of its kind in the US. The OSHbot greets customers, asks them if they need assistance, and guides them to products of interest. It uses natural language technology, and features two rectangular screens, for videoconferencing between the shopper and a store's assistant.

Another area of research in this century is the application of robotics to recognition *(see page 63).* In 2000, Sony announced the Sony Dream Robots (SDR). This robot was able to recognize 10 different facial expressions, express emotion through speech and body language, and walk on rough terrain.

After the World Trade Center attack, iRobot Packbots were employed to search through the rubble for humans, living or dead, and for the recovery of personal items.

The first robotics competition, **Sport for the Mind**, aimed at 9th to 12th graders, combined the excitement of sport with the rigors of science and technology. Under strict rules, limited resources, and time limits, teams of 25 students or more were challenged to raise funds, design a team "brand," hone teamwork skills, and build and program robots to perform prescribed tasks against a field of competitors. Winners qualified for over $19 million in college scholarships.

Facial recognition in the 2010s has found many useful applications. It perhaps was first employed for commercial use at many airports throughout the world for the primary purpose of curbing illegal immigration.

Research into facial recognition actually began in computers in the mid-sixties, and was used for mapping features in photographs and comparing the "map" to other photographs.
These biometrics are now widely used in security systems, and stored in recognition databases along with fingerprint or eye iris metrics.
Combining facial, fingerprint and eye iris biometrics is a powerful tool to identify a single unique person.

Eventually, robots moved into space. A **robotic spacecraft** has no humans aboard and is usually under *telerobotic*[4] control.

In 2001, MD Robotics of Canada launched the Space Station Remote Manipulator System which was used to assemble the International Space Station.

---

[4] Telerobotics is an area of semi-autonomous robotics where spacecraft are controlled either wirelessly or tethered.

A *telemanipulator* is a device that is controlled remotely by a human operator. However, if a device has the ability to perform some autonomous work and some work controlled by a human, it is called a *telerobot*. Finally, if a device is completely autonomous, it is called a robot.

Examples of autonomous or semi-autonomous robots are:
- o Honda's Advanced Step in Innovative Mobility (ASIMO).
- o TOSY's Ping Pong Playing Robot (TOPIO).
- o Industrial robots, also called swarm robots.
- o Microscopic nano robots, sometimes imbedded in animals or humans.
- o Bio-inspired Robots, inspired by nature.

Today's robots typically have the capability to move around in their environment and are not bound to a physical location. However, industrial robots are usually fixed to an assembly position and have a jointed arm and an end effector *(such as a gripper).*

This chapter would not be complete without mentioning laparoscopic robot surgery machines. The forerunner in this field is the Da Vinci Surgical System, produced by Intuitive Surgical.

2030 – Will Computers Become Human?

How about using robots to bring shelves to "pickers" rather than having stock pickers walk up and down the aisles of massive warehouses to collect items listed on a pick list? Amazon has done just that.

In 2012, Amazon purchased Kiva Systems for $775 million. After the acquisition, Amazon stopped selling the Kiva robots to other companies so that they could focus on customizing the robots to move about their warehouses without bumping into each other or other objects.

The result was orange, wheeled objects that bring 4' x 6' shelving units to workers, who pick from the shelves in one position to gather products for specific orders, and place them in bins on a conveyor belt. The bins are received by workers who box and label the goods, and send them to trucks for delivery. The order in which each truck is loaded is consistent with their routes.

Each Kiva now picks and scans 300 items per hour, as compared to 100 under the old system. The cost of sorting, picking and boxing an order has been reduced 20% to 40%. Workers no longer walk up to 20 miles a day to pick orders. Fulfillment costs have reduced dramatically.

The future of robotics is boundless

- Google has developed tiny magnetic particles that can patrol the human body for signs of cancer and other diseases. These nanoparticles, one-thousandth the width of red blood cells, will seek out and attach themselves to cell or proteins inside the body. These magnetic "nanobots" will also carry drugs into the brain.
- The Robat is a robotic wing that helps biologists uncover the secret of bat flight.
- Childlike humanoid robots are now starting to comprehend spoken language.
- Ping Pong ball-sized robots will swarm together to collectively form a smart liquid.
- Animal-shaped "bluffs" can lure predators to a false location, which may be used to divert preying animals and even terrorists.
- Polaris is a solar-powered ice-drilling lunar Prospector-Bot.
- Georgia Tech's 'MacGyver' robots improvise based upon their environment and have been used in search and rescue.
- Robotic sea turtles will carry cargo in their shells.

II-4. Drones

Drones are unmanned aerial vehicles with no onboard crew. They can be remotely piloted or autonomous[5]. They are powered by jets, reciprocating engines, electric engines and may soon be solar-powered.

When employed for military use, drones differ from cruise missiles in that drones are recovered after a mission, while cruise missiles impact their targets and are destroyed. A drone may carry fire munitions, while a cruise missile *is* a munition.

The first recorded use of drones was in 1849 when Austrians attacked Venice, Italy using unmanned balloons loaded with explosives.

Drones have evolved in warfare so that human pilots would not risk their lives in missions. During World War I, the U.S. Navy hired Elmer Sperry, the inventor of the gyroscope, to design and produce unmanned biplanes that could be launched by a catapult, fly over enemy positions and drop "air torpedoes" on the enemy.

In 1938, the Navy experimented with radio-controlled aircraft that were remotely controlled from another aircraft.

[5] The **definition** of **autonomous** is a person or entity that is self-controlling and not governed by outside forces.

In 1941, "Project Fox" was an assault drone with an RCA TV camera in the drone and a TV Screen in the control aircraft. This assault drone successfully torpedoed a German destroyer from 20 miles away.

In World War II, the Navy launched a program called Operation Anvil. The refitted B-24 bombers were filled to capacity with explosives and guided by remote control to crash on selected German targets. These controls were crude radio devices linked to motors in the plane's cockpit.

Unfortunately, Operation Anvil was a disaster, mainly because human pilots were required for take-off, guide the plane to a cruising altitude, and subsequently need to parachute to safety in England. Many planes crashed before the pilot escaped. The most famous victim was John F. Kennedy's older brother Joseph, one of the program's first pilots. It's ironic that the target of Joseph Kennedy's mission was a Nazi site where scientists were thought to be working on technology that would support the remote delivery of explosives.

2030 – Will Computers Become Human?

With advances in precise rocketry, the development of drones stagnated through the fifties. Advances in cruise missiles were more guidable and could take off and maintain altitude with their stubby little wings.

By the late fifties, the success of targeted drones led to their use in other missions, such as reconnaissance. These drones were used to spy on North Vietnam, Communist China and North Korea in the sixties and seventies.

By the end of the fifties, the only U.S. spy plane active was the U-2. It was a single-engine high altitude aircraft operated by the Air Force. They were not drones, however, and were flown by highly trained pilots. In 1960, Gary Powers was shot down over the Soviet Union by a surface to air missile.

Unmanned aerial vehicles were used extensively in the eighties. Their reputation improved dramatically with the Israeli Air Force's victory over the Syrian Air Force in 1982. Israel destroyed dozens of Syrian aircraft with few losses. These drones were used as decoys and electronic signal jammers as well as for video reconnaissance.

After 9/11, the CIA encouraged the use of armed drones for military operations rather than for surveillance. This led to the ethical and management controversy over who was allowed to "pull the trigger".

2030 – Will Computers Become Human?

Drones for the masses

Between 2011 and 2014, China's SZ DJI Technology Company has emerged as the world's largest (by revenue) consumer drone manufacturer. In 2014 it has sold thousands of its 2.8 pound, square footprint devices for about $1000 each.

Almost anyone can pilot DJI's Phantom. With four helicopter-like propellers, it can hover, climb, descend and view terrain below with its high-definition camera.

To target a higher-end professional market, DJI is currently developing its next drone, the Inspire.

Humanitarian groups have used the Phantom to search for survivors after natural disasters. The militant group ISIS has used this drone to for surveillance in Syria.

Phantoms are the top choice of entrepreneurs and producers who use them for filmmaking, construction and farming. Their use is mostly in defiance of the Federal Aviation Administration's moratorium on commercial drones, primarily because it is difficult to regulate and enforce. The FAA plans to propose rules governing the commercial sector by the end of 2014.

As a safety measure, the Phantom is programmed not to fly higher than 985, and uses GPS to prevent it from being used near airports. Legislation is currently underway to restrict commercial drones to very limited use, including the requirement that drones be in view of the person controlling it (i.e., the "pilot").

The future of drones

Tom Frey, Google's esteemed futurist, suggests that in the near future, a video projector mounted in a flying drone could be used to produce special effects at outdoor concerts, or in large stadiums. The projectors could roam around producing spot advertisement, or even subliminal advertising. They could be used for search and rescue to guide lost souls out of a forest, by projecting arrows on the ground. Flying drones could even mask images of humans, to disguise them.

In November 2014, the National Transportation Safety Board (NTSB) ruled that drones are aircraft and are subject to aviation laws, administered by the Federal Aviation Administration (FAA). This ruling is a major victory for the FAA, which has struggled to regulate the rapidly increasing use of drones in the United States.

II-5. Speech Recognition – Audrey to Siri

The development of speech recognition technology over the years is comparable to watching a baby's progress from baby-talk to speaking in syllables like "Mama" and "Dada", to building a large spontaneous vocabulary, and then sprinkling words with wit, humor and inspiration.

At the beginning, speech recognition devices understood only numbers. Then, in 1952, Bell Labs developed the **Audrey** system, which recognized digits spoken by a single voice, after significant "training".

Ten years later, IBM demonstrated its "Shoebox", a machine that could understand sixteen words spoken in English by some persons, but not by others with accents or unusual pitch.

Research labs sprung up in the late sixties in England, Japan, the Soviet Union and the United States. Scientists in these labs invented hardware capable of responding to words that contained four vowels and nine consonants. Speech recognition took off following the advances in the fifties and sixties, when computing was done primarily by primitive mainframe computers.

Not surprising, the U.S. Department of Defense spurred significant growth in speech recognition, through its DARPA[6] Speech Understanding Research (SUR) program. Out of this program evolved Carnegie-Mellon's "Harpy" speech "understanding" program, which could understand over 1000 words, which can be equated to the vocabulary of a 3-year-old.

What is most interesting about speech recognition research from that time is that scientists began to realize that the theory of speech recognition is very closely related to advances in search methodology. This led to the evolution of Siri's voice recognition and response system with Google's search engine methodology. Of course, Siri is more "pure" *(in 2014)* because her responses are unbiased, while Google's search engine results are "ranked" based upon advertising dollars, and somewhat controlled by the effectiveness of search engine optimization.

---

[6] Defense Advanced Research Projects Agency

2030 – Will Computers Become Human?

In the eighties, speech recognition focused on predicting intelligent responses, and faster processing speeds resulted in recognizable vocabulary of several thousand words. Today, it has the potential to recognize an unlimited number of words, in many languages, and can even translate from one language to another.

In 1982, Ray Kurzweil's company, Applied Intelligence and Dragon Systems, released speech recognition applications. By 1985, this software had a vocabulary of 1,000 words. Two years later, in 1987, its lexicon reached 20,000 words, entering the realm of human vocabularies, which range from 10,000 to 150,000 words. But accuracy was only 10% in 1993. Two years later, the error rate crossed below 50%. Dragon Systems released "Naturally Speaking" in 1997, which recognized normal human speech. Progress accelerated primarily due to improved computer performance and larger source text databases. Recently, Kurzweil has collaborated with Google to produce remarkable advances in speech and image recognition.

The "Hidden Markov model", developed by L.E. Baum and his coworkers, applies mathematical algorithms to model language. These statistical models produce a sequence of symbols and quantities that translate sounds to uniform 10-millisecond signals. They can be trained automatically and improve with usage.

These algorithms use context dependency to respond based upon the environment in which the signals are produced. And, as witnessed with Siri and GPS guidance, the voice can be associated with a single responder, male or female.

The future of Speech Recognition

Speech recognition software technology has made incredible advances in recent years, particularly when imbedded in cell phones. Witness the explosion of people using Apple's Siri, or Samsung's counterpart S Voice.

Speech recognition Bluetooth software in automobiles has improved dramatically. High-end cars like Mercedes and BMW are delivered with separate voice command User Manuals and, in the Mercedes the driver is encouraged to use voice commands rather than push buttons. Coupled with integrated phone calling and phone books, speech recognition has made driving safer and reduced accidents caused by distractions such as texting while driving.

2030 – Will Computers Become Human?

Speech recognition and triggered announcements prompted by events in one's calendar, or simply a person's location, is now embedded as a "personal assistant" that assists active people in their day-to-day activities. Voice recognition can be used in apps that control your thermostat, view rooms in your home, turn off lights and close garage doors, and remotely program your DVR.

In the future, expect voice recognition systems to become more conversational and to "remember" your questions and conversations in the past. You won't need to call a specific restaurant to make a reservation. Instead, you'll tell Siri to "make a reservation for two this evening at our favorite Afghan restaurant at the usual time".

Nuance Communications Dragon Software, the mind of Siri, is used heavily in business to reduce interaction of callers with human employees. It is commonplace in call centers, where callers must navigate through a series of menus and, in many cases, never speak to a human, either because they have gotten the response that they were seeking, or because they hang up in frustration.

II-6. Ray Kurzweil: <u>Singularity</u>

In 2005, inventor and futurist Ray Kurzweil wrote a non-fiction book about artificial intelligence and the future of humanity. His book, ***The Singularity Is Near: When Humans Transcend Biology*** *inspired me to write this book.*

Some of the ideas and predictions herein were derived from Kurzweil's previous books, ***The Age of Spiritual Machines*** (1999), and ***The Age of Intelligent Machines*** (1990).

His hypothesis is that with accelerating increases in the performance and capacity of computers, along with vast repositories for data "in the clouds", the world will witness a ***technological singularity***, where machine intelligence will be as powerful as human intelligence. While Kurzweil originally predicted that this singularity would occur in 2045, he subsequently adjusted his prediction to occur on or before 2030.

As this singularity approaches, the human body will be augmented by genetic alterations, nanotechnology, and artificial intelligence imbedded within. This is characterized by Kurzweil as an epoch where human technology and human intelligence merges.

The countdown to technological singularity can be portrayed graphically as the relationship of a particular computer's power[7] to brains of various animals, and ultimately the human, over time.

This achievement is possible because of the converging advances in genetics, nanotechnology, robotics and artificial intelligence. Kurzweil feels that eventually technology will make it possible to maintain the body indefinitely, reverse aging and cure cancer, heart disease and deathly diseases such as Ebola.

In 2012, Kurzweil published **How to Create a Mind.** In it, he describes the brain and correlates the mind to the computer. His book attempts to convince the reader that it is within our reach to create non-biological intelligence that will soar past our own. Of particular interest in this book is the statement that the target for a full brain simulation now moves closer, to 2023.
IBM research in 2014 certainly affirms that direction; see Chapter **II-8. True North - The Brain on a Chip** on page 81.

---

[7] Power as measured in the number of MIPS available for $1,000, closely adhering to Moore's Law.

Assuming that Singularity will indeed occur in or before 2030, , I predict that there will be differences between the human brain and the "brain on a chip", even though the efficacy of Turing's **Imitation Game** results *(see page 42)* will be questioned less and less.

What will the differences be?

- The human response will be based in part on emotions, intuition, involuntary action and ability to recall, while...
- The computer's "brain" will produce a response based upon its knowledge base, total recall and logical decision-making algorithms.
- Human decisions may be based partly upon a person's ethics or fears of consequences, while...
- The computer will make a decision based purely on logic and its knowledge base.
- Humans may consider their rights and responsibilities when they use information available to them, particularly on the Internet, while...
- The computer has no conscience and will not be swayed by ethics, legal concerns, religious beliefs or fear.

2030 – Will Computers Become Human?

- The computer's knowledge base is expected to contain accurate and timeless information, while...
- The information available to a human may be the result of collaborate efforts *(see Wikipedia)* which may have been tainted by conflicting contributions, or contain targeted advertising *(some of which may be subliminal)*, or is just simply incorrect.

What if the computer is <u>more</u> intelligent than humans ?

Kurzweil predicts a time when all the computers in the world will have an aggregate intelligence that is more powerful than all human intelligence combined. He claims that intelligence will then radiate outward from the planet until it saturates the universe, maybe around 2045.

II-7. Movies Humanize the Computer

As far back as 1968, movies have attempted to humanize and "personalize" the computer. Many of the early movies were not based upon technological advances, but were instead mostly science fiction. In 1996, two Stanford professors, Byron Reeves and Clifford Nass, published the results of various psychological studies that suggested that people treat computers, television and media as real people and real places. We even treat computers with female voices differently from computers with male voices.

"2001: A Space Odyssey"

In **1968**, the film ***2001: A Space Odyssey*** hit the big screen. Produced and directed by Stanley Kubrick, the movie was partially inspired by Arthur C. Clarke's short story "The Sentinel". An early draft of the film's scenario was written by both Kubrick and Clarke. This scenario was mostly improvised, rather than based upon the traditional development of a script.

The movie was astoundingly prescient. It revolutionized science fiction and the art of cinematography. It transformed the way we think about film, by introducing revolutionary special effects, a unique narrative style, philosophical undertones and unusual choices of classical musical score such as The Blue Danube, by Johann Strauss II.

2030 – Will Computers Become Human?

A relative unknown, Keir Dullea was offered the lead *(Dr. Dave Bowman)* in the movie.

Because Kubrick was afraid to fly, he remained in London, while the Dawn of Man sequence was being filmed as all still shots *(i.e., photographs)* by his second unit in Africa. The crew communicated with Kubrick in London by land line until he got all the shots that he wanted. The still shots were used as backdrops for the movie, and ape-man actors (mimes) performed live in front of these backdrops.

The story deals with a series of encounters between ape-like humans and tapirs that results in one party being driven off. Next morning, a tall, thin, rectangular black monolith is seen among the rocks. It is soon determined that an alien force moving through our planetary system has dropped the monolith upon the apes' water hole, and war breaks out. One ape's pitching of a bone toward the monolith strikes another bone; this event is considered to be a turning point in our evolution: humanoids learn to kill and hunt with weapons, and to walk upright.

The spinning bone segues to spaceships above Earth, and the Monolith on the Moon section of the movie begins.

Thematically, the film deals with elements of human evolution, technology, artificial intelligence and extraterrestrial life.

2001-A Space Odyssey is notable for its scientific accuracy, pioneering special effects, and minimal use of dialogue.

The spaceship Discovery, 80 million miles above earth, is commanded by Dave Bowman and BBC news is reported on Earth. There are five humans aboard, but three astronauts are in hibernation to save air and food; they will be needed at the destination for a survey.

The sixth member of the crew is the HAL9000 computer, which can talk and mimic the human brain. The BBC newscaster interviews Dave and Frank together and then speaks to Hal, who states he is foolproof and incapable of error.

This is where Hal starts to exhibit human traits, including self-confidence, superiority and stubbornness. Frank and Hal play chess and, of course, Hal wins. Dave sketches and shows his artwork to Hal. HAL expresses some concern about the mission and secrecy. Hal then announces there is a problem with the AE-35 unit and it will fail with 100% certainty within 72 hours.

2030 – Will Computers Become Human?

HAL's confidence and superiority is evidenced by the following excerpts of dialogue from the movie:

HAL: "I am putting myself to the fullest possible use, which is all I think that any conscious entity can ever hope to do".

[*Regarding the supposed failure of the parabolic antenna on the ship, which HAL himself falsified*]
HAL: "It can only be attributable to human error".

Dave Bowman: "Open the pod bay doors, HAL".
HAL: "I'm sorry, Dave. I'm afraid I can't do that".
Dave Bowman: "What are you talking about, HAL?"
HAL: "This mission is too important for me to allow you to jeopardize it".
Dave Bowman: "I don't know what you're talking about, HAL".
HAL: "I know that you and Frank were planning to disconnect me, and I'm afraid that's something I cannot allow to happen".

Dave Bowman: "HAL, I won't argue with you anymore! Open the doors!"
HAL: "Dave, this conversation can serve no purpose anymore. Goodbye".

[*on Dave's return to the ship, after HAL has killed the rest of the crew*]
HAL: "Look Dave, I can see you're really upset about this. I honestly think you ought to sit down calmly, take a stress pill, and think things over".

[HAL's shutdown – starting to exhibit fear]

HAL: "I'm afraid. I'm afraid, Dave. Dave, my mind is going. … My mind is going. There is no question about it. I can feel it. I can feel it. … I'm afraid".

[HAL *gradually slows down and, at the end, sings "Daisy"*]
HAL: "Good afternoon, gentlemen. I am a HAL 9000 computer. I became operational at the H.A.L. plant in Urbana, Illinois on the 12th of January 1992. My instructor was Mr. Langley, and he taught me to sing a song. If you'd like to hear it I can sing it for you".

Kubrick encouraged people to explore their own interpretations of the film, and refused to offer an explanation of "what really happened" in the movie, preferring instead to let audiences embrace their own ideas and theories.

2030 – Will Computers Become Human?

"Her"

Let's compare the humanization of HAL in **2001: A Space Odyssey** (1968) with Samantha in "**Her**" (2013).

Spike Jonze's soulful sci-fi drama "Her" is about Theodore Twombly *(Joaquin Phoenix),* a loner who works as a writer of computer generated handwritten letters for clients.

Theodore purchases a new state-of-the-art computer with the ability to learn and grow with the user. He falls in love with his computer's highly advanced operating system with built-in artificial intelligence, featuring the husky and seductive voice of beautiful actress Scarlett Johansson, but with no image of her. Instead, the viewer sees Samantha as a red screen with a spiral

Meanwhile, reluctant to sign the papers that will finalize his divorce from his childhood sweetheart, a depressed Theodore has slowly withdrawn from his supportive social circle, which includes his longtime friend Amy (Amy Adams), herself floundering in a failed marriage.

Adopting the name Samantha, the perceptive and emotional "software" gradually brings Theodore out of his shell. Soon, their relationship becomes intimate.

Their contributions to the relationship are mutual. Theodore teaches Samantha what it means to feel human, while Samantha gives him the strength to walk away from his failed marriage.

However, conflicts and complications soon arise, when Samantha's rapidly accumulating knowledge base begins to alter the very core of their relationship, and Theodore learns that Samantha has many other relationships.

Some reviewers view this movie as artificial intelligence with a romantic lead. It takes place in a somewhat futuristic Los Angeles, sprawling with skyscrapers, where subways and trains have supplanted the automobile. It projects a "green" society, where most of the world's social maladies, except loneliness, have been reduced or eliminated.

What emerges is Samantha herself, a complex, mature and full-bodied character without a body. explores intimacy between two seemingly human characters, yet only one is human. Although much is left to the viewer's imagination, nothing is lost in the viewer's delight.

The uplifting message from this movie is that a Samantha in the near future may be employed to bring troubled, lonesome introverts out of isolation and into a world of interactive sociability.

II-8. Autonomic Computing

Tremendous advances have been made in the past decade in autonomic computing. An autonomic computing system is a system with sensory input that mimics human senses[8], a knowledge base, a dedicated purpose *(its operating system),* and responses *(effectors)* as output.

Autonomic systems are:

- Self-managing - the system monitors itself.
- Self-configuring - it configures itself automatically.
- Self-optimized - Complex middleware sets its own tunable parameters.
- Self-improving - seeks ways to improve their operations.
- Self-healing - Identifies the root cause of its failures and is adaptive.
- Self-protected - defends the system as a whole against large-scale problems arising from malicious attacks.

Autonomic systems are **not** Drones, which must be remotely controlled by a human being.

---

[8] The least of which is taste.

Autonomic computers are self-managing and adapt to unpredictable changes while masking the intrinsic complexity that operates them. They are capable of building knowledge *(policies)* based upon their environment, ultimately reducing barriers that existed at their initial launch.

As autonomic devices become more complex and capable, predictions in 2014 are that their number will grow by 40% each year. They will continue to be automatic, adaptive and aware, but with increasing capability and purpose.

The Google self-driving vehicle

One of the most fascinating breakthroughs in autonomic computing is Google's self-driving vehicle. Since it must "know" its location, GPS guidance, Google Maps and Google Street View are closely linked to its capability and safe use.

As of 2014, as a result of extensive testing covering nearly every street in Mountain View, the company's 20 or so autonomous vehicles have developed an abiding sense of caution.

2030 – Will Computers Become Human?

Google's cars on freeways tend to leave a shorter distance between themselves and the vehicles they follow than some driver-training manuals recommend, to discourage other motorists from darting dangerously into the space. And when it is their turn to proceed at a four-way stop, Google's cars inch forward decisively in order to prevent other drivers to beat them through the intersection.

Driverless cars have been a dream for decades, largely as a way to reduce the disasters on the roads. About 35,000 people die of crashes in the U.S. annually, with 90 percent of the accidents due to human error, according to the National Safety Council. Google believes its autos could avoid many such mistakes. Many experts believe the vehicles could be bunched together without risk of colliding, reducing traffic congestion and boosting productivity.

It is predicted that, by 2035, 75 percent of vehicles sold worldwide will have some autonomous capabilities, such as being able to park themselves or drive at least part of a trip on autopilot.

Getting these vehicles to the point where they need no human intervention will be a major challenge. It is unclear who would be liable if a self-driving car caused an accident. Company co-founder Sergey Brin has predicted that the Google self-driving vehicle could be commercially available as early as 2017. However, their use would probably be restricted to limited areas for ridesharing or other services, which could operate the cars more economically than individual consumers.

II-9. True North - The Brain on a Chip

In August 2014, IBM announced that its **Almaden Research Center** has delivered its True-North SyNAPSE Chip, a programmable "neurosynaptic" computer chip, the size of a postage stamp, with 5.4 billion transistors, one million programmable neurons, 256 million programmable synapses, and capable of 46 billion "synaptic" operations per second per watt.

This technology could transform science, technology, business, government and society. The IBM team envisions a world populated with sensors that could process data at the speed of the human brain.

The result is architecture on silicon that mimics the human brain. It was funded by a $53.5 million research grant from DARPA. Like the brain, the SyNAPSE is event-driven and enables vision, auditory, and other multi-sensory applications. It operates in biological real time, while consuming a minuscule 70mW, an order of magnitude less power than a modern microprocessor; it runs on the energy equivalent of a hearing-aid battery.

It is expected that, when imbedded in drones, the SyNAPSE will result in a more refined perception of the environment, bringing cognitive computers to society. The result is low-power computing to solve problems in sensing and movement, something that digital computers do awkwardly.

IBM's team member Dharmendra Modha, co-author of a study outlining the chip's development, describes it as "a new machine for a new era." He believes that researchers now have the capability to design a computer that is as efficient as the human brain. True North diverts from traditional "von Neumann" digital computer architecture and more closely mimics the brain's neural functions by having a core driven only when an electrical charge reaches a specific value.

The future use of this chip is limitless. It is ideal for recognition, and could be used in security devices to for facial recognition. It has incredible potential: it could be used in glasses for the visually impaired, implanted in the ears of the partially deaf or the eyes of the partially blind, and used in medical imaging to detect early signs of disease. It can improve the capabilities of driverless vehicles.

It is expected that True-North SyNAPSE Chip chip will have artificial intelligence characteristics when it is to change based upon its experience. In other words, it will have the ability to learn.

2030 – Will Computers Become Human?

II-10. Wearable Technology

As processors become faster, and a proliferation of portable devices for consumers expands dramatically into the marketplace, many devices which previously were carried, are being worn instead.

The Apple Watch

A groundbreaking announcement by Scott Cook, Apple's CEO at their September 2014 iPhone 6 event was the introduction of the **Apple Watch**.

Expected to be priced starting at $349 when released in 2015, it is packed with features which will undoubtedly capture the minds and pocketbooks of consumers:

> **Communication**
> - Digital Touch. Users can draw quick images and send them to their friends.
> - Emoji. Similar to emoticons on the phone. However, they can be customized and animated.
> - Receive Calls and Text. It is compatible with the iPhone 5 and beyond. When text is received, it is analyzed and the watch suggests replies.

- o <u>Walkie-talkie</u>. Used to send short voice messages, it is probably far advanced from Dick Tracy's 2-Way Wrist Radio of 1946.
- o Wi-Fi. Built in to communicate with the iPhone.

> **Fitness**
>   - o Measures heart rate.
>   - o Accelerometer. Counts your steps, calculates calories burned, and measures total body activity[9].
> **App development**. A tool called the WatchKit is available for developers who create third-party apps.
> **iTunes and Apple TV access**. Listen to iTunes radio.
> **Siri**. On the watch, it integrates with the Maps feature to provide guided directions.
> **Apple Pay**. A virtual wallet that digitizes and encrypts bank transactions.

---

[9] It will most likely be tied in to fitness apps like **Map my Walk.**

2030 – Will Computers Become Human?

Google Glass

The Google Glass is an optical head-mounted display intended to explode into the marketplace as a wearable hands-free device. It communicates "in the clouds" with natural language voice commands. Google Glass was introduced with a choice of four prescription frames to which the device can be attached.

Developed at the same Google X facility that produces the driverless car, Google Glass was test-marketed in 2013 by inviting interested users to use the Twitter hashtag #ifihadglass. In order to qualify as an early purchaser of the product, customers were invited to pay $1500 for the product and attend a demonstration in one of three major cities in the U.S.

Google Glass features a touchpad, a camera for taking photos or videos, and a liquid-crystal display reflected into the wearer's eye. Several third-party apps are available for facial recognition, exercise, photo manipulation and sharing.

Many concerns have been raised about privacy, safety, etiquette and the ethics of using the device in public.
There is much controversy over its potential success. While many reviewers call it life-changing, others feel that, once all its features have been tried, it proves of little usefulness and becomes just a novelty item.

The wearable technology market is exploding, with innovative and original ideas. It will not be difficult to attract consumers to so some of these new items, if not for their useful purpose, then at least for their latest fashion statement.

Some of the innovative technology to hit the market in 2014 is the Jawbone Up24, the Withings Pulse O2 , the Pebble Steel, the Misfit Shine, the Fitbit Zip, AiQ Smart Clothing, the Garmin Vivofit, and   robotic fabric. Are they in your wardrobe?

2030 – Will Computers Become Human?

II-11. Will Computers Become Human?

So when does a computer really become human?
As Turing suggested in his, it is probably when a
computer or device cannot be distinguishable
from a human *(at least if they are not seen).*

The most important characteristics of a computer[10]
that make it indistinguishable from a human are:

- ❖ **Emotional Detection –it** detects
  happiness, sadness, anger, fear, surprise,
  and disgust.
- ❖ **Sensory Capability –** it is "aware" and
  can receive stimuli from sensors that
  "effect" actions or responses.

It is not necessary for this humanized computer
to have a processor such as the True North chip
that simulates the brain. However, emotions and
senses are likely to be present on a PC's typical
chip.

How will advances in technology produce
computers with emotions? Scientists and
researchers are making advances in emotional
artificial intelligence, which is also called affective
computing.

Researchers have developed facial recognition
software that can recognize emotions in students

[10] In this chapter, a "computer" is any autonomic device.

such as frustration, confusion or boredom, and use these observations to improve the quality of education and educators.

Google's Futurist in Chief, Ray Kurzweil, is involved with *semantic search*, where advanced search algorithms can "understand" the context and intentions of a query, which can result in a conversation between the user and her computer.

Kurzweil says *"I've had a consistent date of 2029 for that vision.. And that doesn't just mean logical intelligence. It means emotional intelligence, being funny, getting the joke, being sexy, being loving, understanding human emotion. That's actually the most complex thing we do. That is what separates computers and humans today. I believe that gap will close by 2029."*

There are parallel developments in this area of research. **Affectiva** has developed facial recognition software that analyzes expressions and physiological responses in order to detect human feelings. An Israeli company, **Beyond Verbal**, determines emotions based upon human sounds and tone of voice. Microsoft's Kinect tracks players' heartbeats and physical movements when playing games to gain insight about how people feel when they play those games.

Humanoid robots, like the **Nao** not only react to emotions, but learn to imitate them.

2030 – Will Computers Become Human?

Scientists at MIT have constructed a robot with a synthetic head and movable eyelids, eyes and lips. Parents are invited to play with Kismet, who initially looks sad, but smiles when it detects a human face. If the parent moves too fast, Kismet expresses fear.

Imagine if you sat down at your computer and it could recognize your emotional state using facial recognition software. Knowing that you are sad, the computer might try to lighten you up by making a joke. Your computer might even ignore you when you are irritable until it knows that you have had a cup of coffee, or have been kissed by your spouse.

As noted in "Her", a computer can fall in and out of love, or be jealous, even if it doesn't have a body.

Epilogue

This book, the first in my "**30**" series, is based, for the most part, upon history, the results of research, established technology and the inventions of scientists, researchers and engineers. However, the composite of all this work is strictly my speculation.

My next book, **2060 – A Neural Odyssey**, will compile the conclusions, predictions and dreams of visionaries, futurists, technologists and dreamers. Could networks of machines dominate human society?

My third yet-to-be-named book, **2090 - ????**, will be a work of fiction, based partly on Kurzweil's prediction that intelligence will radiate outward from our planet until it saturates the universe.

ABOUT THE AUTHOR

After graduating from the U.S. Coast Guard Academy with a degree in Marine Engineering, Pete served as an officer on several assignments in the Pacific and in California. During his six years in the Coast Guard, he was Commanding Officer of two Coast Guard units.

His information technology career includes systems design and development positions at IBM, Electronic Data Systems and Chevron. Pete served in several project management roles designing, developing and managing major financial systems projects at Chevron and Household Financial Services.

Presently, Pete provides business consulting services to businesses, large and small, in many industries. His focus is in integrating his clients' applications seamlessly with company web sites and other installed business applications. Many of Pete's clients are wineries. He also serves manufacturers and distributors with complex inventory management requirements.

Pete is the Leader of the San Francisco Bay Area Group of the National Advisors Network (NAN). NAN's sole purpose is to empower Intuit-certified QuickBooks ProAdvisors.

Pete is consumed by advances in artificial intelligence, voice recognition and developments in computer chips that mimic the brain.

Index